Buy Signals
Sell Signals

Strategic Stock Market Entries and Exits

By Steve Burns & Holly Burns

www.NewTraderU.com

Table of Contents

Disclaimer

This book is meant to be informational and should not be used as trading advice. All traders should gather information from multiple sources, and create their own trading systems. The authors make no guarantees related to the claims contained herein. Please trade responsibly.

Version 2015.10.22

Trading price action instead of fundamentals

"When I got into the business, there was so little information on fundamentals, and what little information one could get was largely imperfect. We learned just to go with the chart. Why work when Mr. Market can do it for you?" – Paul Tudor Jones

Fundamental analysis is the examination of the underlying forces that affect the well being of the economy, industry groups, and companies. As with most analysis, the goal is to derive a forecast and profit from future price movements. - Definition courtesy of StockCharts.com

Technical Analysis is the examination of current and past behavior of participants that are buying and selling a particular financial market based on price action. The goal of technical analysis is to find patterns in price action that are profitable.

More than twenty years ago, my father-in-law bought a used truck that he wanted to flip for a quick profit. He looked at the mileage on the odometer, the condition, the make, model, age, and the fact that it was a stick shift, and decided on a price based on all these factors. I thought his price was high because there were plenty of used trucks in the world and not a lot of buyers looking for this particular type.

He asked me what I thought the value of the truck was. I thought about it and told him I thought the value of the truck was exactly what he could get someone to pay for it. The value would be established as offers to buy the truck came in, versus his initial sell price.

The suggested value for the truck he would find in books was only a fundamental valuation. The publisher of Kelley Blue Book was not offering to buy the truck, they were giving him a value guideline. The true value would be set by the first person with cash offering to buy his truck.

Values are based on buyers and sellers and not opinions or fundamental valuations. Prices can move so far away from fundamentals that they are useless. Needless to say, my thoughts about technical price action versus the *belief* of value didn't go over great with my former drill sergeant father-in-law. He was not impressed that I would question his wisdom on buying a depreciating asset as an "investment". But he is not unlike the millions of fundamentalist investors in financial markets who get angry when price doesn't align with their belief about value.

Similarly, fundamentalist investors that buy companies based on what they should be worth but can't make money off their investment portfolio during bear markets and downtrends, can become easily frustrated because they have placed their trust in the belief of value.

This book is about trading price action instead of investing in a company based on its balance sheet and stock price versus book value. The concepts in this book will show you how to create actual trading plans for buying high probability setups, trading on the right side of a trend, and exiting with a profit without having to look at fundamental valuations. This is a book for traders that want to profit from price action and not for investors wanting to buy a company that is undervalued in the hope that one day the true value will be priced in.

There are trading systems that incorporate fundamental valuations like price-to-earnings ratios, return on equity, sales growth, and other metrics that create their watch lists based on fundamentals, but still trade based on technical price action, a trading system, or chart patterns. *Even if you can find the best value stocks or growth stocks to trade, you will only profit if you buy them and sell them at the right time.*

Let price guide your decisions on buying and selling? Inside the investing world this will seem like blasphemy. Regardless of what anyone believes a company is worth, the company and the stock are two different things.

A company is a corporate entity with a profit and loss statement that is charged with making profits for shareholders and making Wall Street happy by beating earnings. Businesses must create earnings by selling goods to customers in an efficient and cost effective way that makes money. Corporate profits end up on the company's balance sheet, which can be used to reinvest in the company through capital expenditures, or to pay a dividend to company shareholders.

The company's stock is all together different, because it trades on an exchange and buyers and sellers determine the price of that stock and what they are *willing* to pay. In my experience, very little buying and selling is based purely on fundamental valuations. Most market action is based on a trader or investor's emotions.

Every buyer and seller has a different motivation for buying or selling. The only rational reason to buy a stock is because you think that the stock is going to go up in price and you will make money. Even when short sellers buy a stock back to cover their short position, it is because they want to lock in their profits before the stock goes higher.

While there is only one reason to buy a stock, people will sell a stock for many different reasons:

- They need the cash.
- They see a better investment or trade.
- They are fearful that the price will go down.
- A mutual fund manager has to sell holdings to raise cash.
- They believe the future of the company is in peril.
- They are fearful about the economy.
- They believe a new technology will disrupt the company.
- Something on the daily news.
- A rumor that is causing the stock to drop.
- They are nearing retirement and changing their portfolio balance.
- They are rebalancing their portfolio by selling positions that have gotten too large.
- The shares are inherited and the heirs prefer cash.

All of these reasons for selling play out every day. None of them required a balance sheet or a price-to-earnings ratio. The markets are largely driven off the decisions of the asset holders rather than fundamental valuations. The buyers and sellers on stock exchanges can be value investors, high frequency traders, trend followers, day traders, swing traders, growth investors, mutual fund managers, or hedge fund managers. All market participants have one motivation: to make money.

Always remember: While there are many reasons to sell a stock there is only one rational reason to buy a stock: because the buyer believes it will go up in value and they can sell it for a profit in the future. The 'future' can be different things to different people. For Warren Buffett the future may be 'never' and for a day trader it could be in 30 minutes.

The only thing that makes stock market participants money is exiting a position with a profit after price moves in their favor. Stock prices are driven by the specific supply and demand of their stock, not by the underlying company's results. It's the perception of the company's current and future results that interests buyers and sellers. A company's stock price has to go through the filter of all the market participants' perceptions, opinions, and predictions about what the current price should be versus what the future price may be.

Fundamental analysis is a long-term game that can last for years. Warren Buffett's success as the greatest investor of all time is not based on simple fundamental value investing. The real key to Buffett's incontrovertible record is based on his ability to create the best margin of safety on his purchases. By picking the right ones the majority of the time, holding a concentrated portfolio of only his best picks, with an unlimited holding period, he has compounded his returns for decades.

One of the keys to his success was acquiring the textile company, Berkshire Hathaway. Initially an aging business model, Buffet converted it into a successful insurance holding company whose insurance premiums could be used to acquire healthy companies with great cash flow, and those with 'moats' around their business models that make it difficult for industry competition.

His patience is legendary, often waiting years for a desired price. His buy signals are often triggered by extreme fear, when stock is available at a large discount. This value ratio creates a margin of safety that limits the downside risk even if he's wrong. His risk/reward ratio offers a significant gain if he's right, and the stock returns to a price that better reflects an accurate fundamental valuation of the company. Warren Buffet rarely sells, but he will exit his holdings when the business conditions are no longer favorable and there is little upside.

Very few people will have the patience, discipline, genius, and luck to be anything like Warren Buffet. However, most people can trade simple price action trading systems on a comfortable timeframe. If they use position sizing correctly, they can handle the emotional issues that hinder the majority of other traders and investors.

Fundamentalists can suffer from long losing streaks. Investors tend to have larger drawdowns in capital and can give back years of returns very quickly during bear markets and financial crises. A good trader will have tight controls over losses, risk exposure, and drawdowns in their capital.

Conservative buy and hold investors have dealt more pain over the past 15 years than most traders experienced with the 2000-2002 bear market, and the 2008-2009 financial crises. Traditional buy and hold investors focused on retirement generally set their buy signals for every payday resulting in a new contribution into their retirement account. Young buy and hold investors not worried about their retirement accounts, look for buy signals all day, every day.

Buy and holder investors generally sell when they are rebalancing their portfolios once a quarter, or annually when they sell their winning positions to use the capital to buy positions that haven't kept up, like bonds or other equity sectors. Another time that they will start selling positions is when they get closer to retirement, as they start to move their portfolios from stocks into lower risk and more stable bonds.

Buy and holders expose themselves to unlimited risk with no stops because their investing system is based in the belief that stocks will have good returns the majority of the time over a ten-year period. This system seems to be more for the benefit of the mutual fund industry than investors. A little later in this book, we will explore some simple trend following systems that easily outperform buy and hold investing with half the drawdowns.

A poignant example of the disconnect between fundamental valuations and stock prices is the Internet bubble of 1999 and 2000, before the price plunge of the tech sector brought it back into balance. The NASDAQ 5000 was an irrational price trend based on the idea that the Internet would change the world and commerce overnight. The Internet has changed the world, but prices were about 15 years ahead of the fundamentals in even the best technology companies. Most of the dot com companies were worthless, but they made millionaires out of traders that traded them based strictly off price action exiting with their profits when prices peaked.

Another excellent example of a complete disconnect between fundamentals and price action was the market meltdown of 2008-2009. Was Ford Motor Company really worth $1? If Ford was worth $1 fundamentally and then went up to almost $19, did the balance sheet reflect this? I was warning friends not to buy Ford all the way from the $9 price level as it kept falling. I didn't examine the balance sheet, but I could see that the chart was in a downtrend, and it was obvious that investors and traders were pricing in a possible bankruptcy of Ford.

Was CitiGroup really fundamentally valued at .97 cents in March 2009? Can investors price in government bailouts with their fundamentals? A price action trader would have used signals to exit before Lehman Brothers, Bear Stearns, and the whole financial sector started melting down. Most fundamental investors lost a lot of money in 2008 and 2009, with no exit strategy from individual stocks or the stock market, and could only watch as a decade of gains disappeared.

I have several problems with fundamental investing. When these investors buy something based on the belief of what it should be worth, it looks even better when the price goes lower and lower. It's also difficult for fundamental investors to know when to exit with a profit. While buy and hold investors in 2015 feel pretty good about themselves for holding through 2008-2009 and getting back to even, those that had sizable accounts from a lifetime of compounding didn't feel so good when they were down 50% of their portfolio in March of 2009 and ready for retirement.

A good trader controlling their risk and position sizing will rarely have to suffer through drawdowns that investors take during corrections and bear markets. As traders, we have exit signals that limit our losses. I had a profitable year in 2008 by following price action. A 50% drawdown in a brokerage account will discourage most people from wanting to trade or invest again. This kind of financial, mental, and emotional pain should be avoided at all cost.

While there are many legendary fundamental investors and fund managers that have found success, there are also wealthy technicians that simply and systematically trade price action. I think that the greatest opportunity for retail traders and small investors is to let the big investors and other market participants place their bets, analyze what they are doing, and follow along. I have been doing this in some form or another in my personal accounts for over 20 years, and it works. You don't have to predict the trend you just have to find ways to ride the wave in the right direction.

There are systematic ways to create buy and sell signals to outperform the market's returns. Even a simple trend filter can dramatically reduce your losses during corrections and bear markets. Regardless of how active you want to be in the stock market, this book can help you. Even fundamentalist investors would do better if they let the fundamentals tell them what to buy, and allow the price action and chart to tell them when to get in and when to get out.

Trading price signals instead of emotional signals

"Dramatic and emotional trading experiences tend to be negative. Pride is a great banana peel, as are hope, fear, and greed. My biggest slip-ups occurred shortly after I got emotionally involved with positions." – Ed Seykota

It is said that over 90% of active traders in the financial markets don't make money over the long-term. There is a lot of confusion about the exact numbers, but it's safe to say that it's difficult to be profitable over time. Even investors have terrible timing on their buy and sell decisions, but why is this the case? It typically comes down to emotions.

The majority of the errors that traders and investors make are emotional ones because they rely on internal signals. Their emotions give birth to a buy and sell strategy that is unproven and often unprofitable. We've witnessed this as many of the wild price swings that make no sense in the current market environment. If you want to make a quantum leap in profitability, the first step is to stop buying or selling anything without a solid, quantifiable, external reason for doing so.

Greed was the primary driver of the NASDAQ 5000 bubble in March of 2000, not the valuations of 'eyeballs' on websites. Buyers continually piled into dot com stocks with no real intrinsic value, and held them due to the greed of more gains and higher highs. The NASDAQ 5000 trend could have been traded profitably with the right entry and exit signals. Simple chart patterns and moving averages made many traders a lot of money in 2000. I had enough money in March of 2000 to pay off my new house when I was 27 years old, and I have been hooked ever since.

The problem during this period was the traders and investors that traded based on their personal euphoria that allowed them to hold their positions during the parabolic tech uptrend, didn't allow them to lock in profits and exit their positions. Using trailing stops would have helped them exit and keep large gains instead of riding their tech stocks all the way back down.

In March of 2009 all major stock indexes made lows that seemed impossible just a year before. The selling escalated because of a fear of holding equities, and sellers were willing to let go at ridiculously low prices. Long-term trend traders should have been out of the long side of stocks and limited losses in 2008 using any reasonable sell.

The easiest sell signal for a trader or investor to use to limit the destruction of their capital is to exit their holdings and go to cash when the S&P 500 index tracking ETF SPY closes under its 200-day simple moving average. For stock indexes, this one simple exit signal decreases drawdowns of capital by about 50% in the past 15 years of backtests. It doesn't increase the returns in most cases, but exiting when the 200-day simple moving average is lost will cut the down side in half.

You have the option to be in cash during market corrections, bear markets, recessions, and market meltdowns, and you can wait to start buying again when the indexes start closing over the 200-day. *This could be the most important signal in this book.* The majority of investors and traders would do well to go to cash when the stock market indexes are trading under the 200-day moving average, and wait for better opportunities on the upside. An index tracking exchange traded fund like SPY, QQQ, IWM, or DIA closing below the 200-day moving average should be your first warning sign of danger.

Pride makes people hold what they thought was a good investment or long side trade even though it has slipped dramatically. The only reason to buy anything is for the possibility of it going up in price. Pride is the signal that keeps a trader in a losing position and unwilling to admit they are wrong. It prevents the use of stop losses and proper exit signals. A trader with too much pride won't even understand the need for exit signals because they are blind to the possibility of being wrong.

Hope is another dangerous signal used by traders. A trader will buy a stock that is falling lower day after day based on the unfounded hope that it will go higher. Hope is not a dip buying signal. A stock index approaching the 30 RSI and above the 200-day moving average on the daily chart during a bull market is a much better buy signal. You must have a quantifiable, external reason to buy a dip that puts the odds in your favor based on price action and not because you hope something good will happen.

Fear is one of the internal trade signals that completely undermine a trader's ability to be profitable. There are two ways to be profitable, have more wins than losses or have big wins and small losses. A high winning percentage system should have wins and losses equal in size to make your system profitable. Likewise, having big wins and small losses can allow even a small winning percentage system to make money, provided there are enough large enough wins. Huge losses will make you unprofitable regardless of big wins or a high winning percentage because you will give back your profits from your winning trades, and eventually destroy your trading capital.

Fear can signal a trader to take a small winning trade while the profits are still there before it disappears, making it difficult to have any big wins. Exit a trade based on a trailing stop, time stop, or because a price target is reached rather than give into your fears. It can also make a trader miss a valid entry signal because they are afraid of losing money.

Greed can believe in your entry signals too much and often wants to trade with too much position size. Greed is confidence gone wrong. Each trade signal you use should be designed to put the odds in your favor, but even a great trade signal is not a guaranteed win, it's just a possibility with a good probability. Many great trading systems only have 60% win rates. The key is how the trader manages to keep the 40% losing trades small while maximizing the winning trades.

Greed can also blind a trader from taking the profits off the table when their profit target is reached. Greed for gains after the risk/reward ratio has skewed against the initial entry can lead to losses when a trend reverses. One of the most expensive things a trader can do is not take profits at their target as the market reverses, instead waiting for the price to recover after it's too late. Greed wants to trade big and stay in winning trades forever. Your trading plan has to override your greed, control position size, and have a strategy to take your profits when they are available.

One of the cornerstones of my teachings is that emotions are terrible trading signals. Emotions want to buy falling knives at the beginning of market corrections and bear markets instead of waiting for the market to find key price support levels. Signals are created to give you a quantifiable reason to do the opposite of what your emotions are telling you to do.

Your trading success will be largely based on your ability to approach the markets in a systematic way using a trading plan to utilize profitable buy and sell signals that fit your market beliefs and methodology. You need a good external guide that you follow regardless of what your emotions are telling you to do. Trade your signals and not your feelings, opinions, or emotions.

Reactive technical analysis versus predictions

"Trend followers are the group of technical traders who use reactive technical analysis. Instead of trying to predict a market direction, their strategy is to react to the market's movements whenever they occur. Trend followers respond to what has happened rather than anticipating what will happen. They strive to keep their strategies based on statistically validated trading rules. This enables them to focus on the market and not get emotionally involved. " – Michael Covel

Traditional technical analysis is based on forecasting future price movements based on past price action. This book is about reacting to current price action. The best traders in the world stay flexible and can change their trades quickly. They can also stay with a winning trade and allow it to trend as far as it will go, capturing huge wins when possible. Reactive technical analysis doesn't exit a winning trade until there is a reason to exit, and it prompts traders to exit losing trades when price action proves them wrong.

One of the worst things you can do is try to predict what will happen next. This is a waste of time and energy, and a great way for a trader to sabotage months or even years of trading profitability. Traders and investors must have pre-set price levels that they will adhere to, so they can realize they are wrong and change their course, rather than losing more money or missing a trend. One of the worst things you can be is a stubborn bull in a bear market or a stubborn bear in a bull market. All traders must have the "I am wrong" signal.

How many times do we see a talking head on financial television or a trader or investor on social media blinded by their own bias? They either have a theory that a market crash is imminent based on some macro economic trends or other outside influence. I don't care what people say or predict will happen, my question is what position do they have right now to prove their beliefs? The most opinionated people you will find typically don't have any current market positions and they are only expressing their opinions. Ignore them. I have found over the years that the profitable traders and investors carry their opinions lightly and their stops tightly. It is easy to hold a bearish opinion about the markets and then while you hold that bias the Dow Jones industrial Average moves 2,000 points up in a few months. If you are in cash, then you have missed a large market move. If you are short, then you have lost a large amount of money. The point of having a signal is to have an external event that forces you to change your position in the right direction.

What if in the summer 2009, a trader was bearish on the chart, and the initial failure to breakout over the 200-day made him believe we were are doomed to return to all-time lows. All he heard was bad news on television and online. He was negative, saw no hope for a rally, and was ready to sell the market short. This is what his chart might look like:

Charts courtesy of StockCharts.com.

What would he need to see to change his bearish bias? From the look of the chart, he had some good reasons to be systematically bearish, and even short. If he was short then, he should have a stop loss level where he would be proven wrong. Maybe a close back over the 200-day moving average would have made him exit his short position. If he was in cash, he would need to know what level would get him short again. A failure at the 200-day moving average and a reversal might make him sell short into strength again.

Here is what I would look for a reversal out of this downtrend and a potential uptrend starting:
- A bullish crossover of the MACD the black line crossing over the red line signaling upside momentum.
- The RSI crossing over the 50 RSI and getting back on the bullish side of the chart.
- Price closing over the 200-day simple moving average showing that the bulls are willing to buy over that line, and that selling could be exhausted below it.
- These are momentum buy signals. We are looking for the market to confirm the beginning of momentum and the start of a new uptrend *before* we enter.

Here is what happened next:

Charts courtesy of StockCharts.com.

I tried to keep this chart as simple and clean as possible so you can see how the signals we were already looking for played out, and how the chart evolved after the entry signals were triggered.

Entry signals are just step one. Managing the trade through position sizing, trailing stops, and targets are part of the bigger picture. We will cover these signals in depth in future chapters, but I wanted to give you your first glimpse of how everything can change in a market, and how you need to be flexible enough to go with the flow.

The quote at the beginning of this chapter is from my friend and trend following expert Michael Covel. He has spent many years studying what makes Trend Followers successful in the markets. Trend Followers create systematic ways to capture trends in financial markets through technical trading rules for entries and exits that put the odds in their favor. This school of thought had the biggest impact on my development as a trader.

While I have evolved my trading for different market environments and shorter time frames, Trend Following principles of reacting instead of predicting has been at the core of my profitability. I have always been adverse to risk, so I had no problem cutting my losses short because I hate to lose money. And because of the bull markets in equities in 2003-2007, it was easy to let my winners run and become very profitable. Most people have little trouble in bull markets, it's when asset values start going down and stay down when the trouble begins.

As technical trader, it is our job to create systematic ways to capture trends on our trading time frame, and we have to let price guide our entries and exits. We are attempting to go with the flow of capital into and out of the market, and develop signals that get us in at the right moment to capture a trend. Our exit signals will get us out when we are proven wrong for a small loss or allow us to lock in profits when it appears the trend is at an end and ready to bend. We aren't trading our emotions, beliefs, or predictions; price action will be our guide on our journey to profitability.

Analyzing a chart to predict what will happen in the future is not the same as looking at current conditions and setting buy and sell signals targets if a price level is reached. Your signal has to be based on the current reality of price and not the future expectations of price.

A systematic approach may not always work in the short-term, but it is designed to keep the odds in your favor so that over the long-term you will be able to capitalize on profitable trends. A price trading system exposes your capital to the opportunity to capture a trend while limiting your losses when wrong. Your position sizing and stop losses will be just as important in your trading system as your entry signals. Your ability to follow your signals will be just as important as the quality of the signals that your create.

Different types of markets (range bound, volatile, trending)

"There is only one side of the market and it is not the bull side or the bear side, but the right side." - Jesse Livermore

Many new traders will pick up a book titled *Buy Signals, Sell Signals* and want to go straight to the signals and trade them. I will share some key signals in this book and how to use them, but there are a few things traders need to understand about signals before they rush into trading.

Please understand that no signals are magic and work at all times, in all markets. This is called the "Search for the Holy Grail" in trading circles, and it is a complete waste of time. No trading signals are profitable in all markets at all times because markets change from trending to not trending, and from not volatile to very volatile. Markets can go from smooth uptrends supported by ascending key moving averages, to range bound with price levels that provide upper resistance and lower support. Markets can trade in a very tight price range day after day and then the daily price range can triple or even quadruple.

Trading is not about magic signals but about putting the odds in your favor with the best entries for the market that you are currently invested in. First, you create valid entry signals that have the potential for putting you on the right side of the trend in your time frame. Then you take your signal when it occurs with the right position size to control risk, and then there is nothing else you can do but let the next market move make you profitable or unprofitable.

Here are the different market environments that a trader and investor will experience.

A range bound market is one that moves inside a fairly defined price range over a certain length of time. It is a market with a price resistance level where current position holders are ready to sell at that resistance level to lock in profits, and possibly wait for lower prices to buy back into the market at a later time. Resistance levels are the price where buyers are not willing to step in and drive prices any higher. Resistance is where buyers lose interest and sellers are ready to lock in profits. Range bound markets have price support levels where current position holders are not willing to sell any lower and buyers are ready to step in and take a position.

While the resistance and support levels are not exact, they usually fall into a very close range and can be defined by horizontal trend lines based on repetitive price action to those levels. Technical indicators can also act as key indicators as resistance or support. For example, the RSI (Relative Strength Index) can signal resistance near the 70 RSI and support at the 30 RSI on the daily chart during range bound environments, especially in stock indexes and big cap stocks.

Buying price weakness and selling price strength are the profitable signals in range bound markets, or said another way, buying near support and selling near resistance. Range bound markets come before and after trends in most cases. The transition from range bound to trending is signaled by price closing above resistance or below support. In many cases, once a price range is broken from the upside the old resistance becomes the new support. When support is lost and a new downtrend begins, old support can become the new resistance. Many trend following trading signals and momentum signals are built on the breakout of trading ranges. Trend and momentum signals are trying to enter when there is a high possibility of a new trend beginning.

When you are drawing horizontal support lines they must always go from left to right. You are looking for a future confirmation of a new trend line. The more touches you have without it being broken, the more valid the resistance or support line becomes. An intra-day breach of a line is not confirmed for me until it closes above or below that line.

In this example, you can see $SPY made a new high in May of 2015, replacing the old resistance as the new price level held as resistance for the next three months. The old resistance held back rallies in late July and August. Two levels of support also put in a floor for lower prices as this market remained range bound. Stock indexes and slow growth big cap stocks tend to stay range bound the majority of the time, while growth stocks and commodities can have very strong trends.

Charts courtesy of StockCharts.com.

Markets in uptrends are defined by higher highs and higher lows. The emotions that dominate bull markets are hope and greed. Often, true bull markets are making new all-time highs in price. The stronger the uptrend, the shorter the moving averages that will support it on pullbacks on the way up. The long-term support for a bull market is typically the 200-day simple moving average. While this line may be lost at times, it is usually regained quickly and the uptrend continues.

Bull Markets have no long-term resistance levels. They consistently make new highs in price. A bull market is caused by an asset class being under accumulation, so when stocks are being accumulated the stock market is in a bull phase. Bull Markets tend to start down in the morning and end up at the end of the day. This is profit taking in the morning and then accumulation in the afternoon. Bull Markets typically end when buyers are exhausted and when the majority has taken their full positions in a market.

Breakout signals and buying dips when price pulls back are typically profitable in bull markets. Uptrends can be very strong due to the lack of selling pressure with stop losses and trailing stops not being hit, and the need for short sellers to continue to cover their short positions at higher prices. The primary selling pressure in bull markets is profit taking.

In this example, you see a clear uptrend on a daily chart during the bull market in 2013. The rising 50-day simple moving average provided the first level of support in this uptrend, and the ascending 100-day simple moving average provided the secondary level of support as this uptrend was confirmed repeatedly.

Charts courtesy of StockCharts.com.

Downtrends are defined by lower highs and lower lows. The emotion that dominates bear markets is fear. Downtrends are not as smooth as uptrends because they are mixed with outsized plunges due to fear and strong rallies due to short covering and dip buying by people trying to catch the bottom. The large drops during downtrends can be triggered by stop losses and trailing stops being hit. This causes a chain reaction of sell orders compounded by short sellers adding fuel to the fire. Bear Markets are caused by the distribution of an asset class. In Bear Markets, the primary signals that work are selling short into strength and buying only the most oversold dips. There are times (in extreme downtrends) when selling short into weakness can work.

Here is an example of Apple stock in a downtrend in the second half of 2012. Notice that the 21 day EMA and the 10-day SMA both acted as descending resistance as Apple made lower lows. It fell quickly from the $700+ level for no fundamental reason. The decline was interrupted by one rally that lasted for 10-days, and then fell back under the downslope moving averages and made fresh lows.

Charts courtesy of StockCharts.com.

These charts are examples of letting the price be your guide in trading the price action on the daily chart. People that traded the chart with the right key moving averages and technical indicators suffered far fewer losses than investors that were stubbornly on the wrong side of downtrends, or traders who had bearish opinions in a bull market.

Remember: Your buy and sell signals are only one third of your trading. You must have the discipline to take your signals when they are triggered, and risk a small amount of your total trading capital on any single trade. No trading system will be profitable if it is not traded with discipline and the right position size and risk management.

- In range bound markets buy signals are near support, and sell signals are at resistance until a range bound breakout changes the chart pattern into a new trend.
- During uptrends, trading signals that will work are buying pullbacks, momentum signals, and breakouts.
- Trend trading buy signals can be a breakout to a new high over a set number of days or weeks.
- Buying gap ups in price can work during Bull Markets with the low of the day as a stop loss.
- Buying a dip can be a signal based on a pullback to a rising short-term moving average like the 21 day or 50-day.
- Momentum signals can be a bullish candlestick over the previous day's high or a gap up that holds the low of day as support over the next few days of trading.
- Signals that work in downtrends are selling short into resistance at the previous day's high price, selling into rallies back to a key declining moving average like the 5-day exponential moving average, or the 200-day simple moving average.
- During bear markets, sometimes selling into declining price weakness when a key technical support level is lost, like the 30 RSI on a daily chart, works because in many markets low prices just get lower.

Additional dynamics to consider

"I think investment psychology is by far the most important element, followed by risk control, with the least important consideration being the question of where you buy and sell." – Tom Basso

This may seem like a strange quote to put in a book that is about when to buy and when to sell, but it is crucial to understand all of the elements that go into successful trading. There is much more to consider than having a good buy and sell system.

The key elements that should partner with your buy and sell signals are position sizing and your risk management principles. You must have an equity curve that you can survive. Most of the traders that don't make it quit because they can't overcome the emotional and financial pain of losing money.

Here are some of the other dynamics that you must navigate to effectively execute your entry and exit signals and achieve profitability:

- Are you able to take the signal you were planning to take when it is triggered?
- Are you able to cut your loss when your stop is initially hit?
- Can you control your position size on your entry, and not trade too big when emotions get the best of you?
- Can you resist the desire to add to a losing trade because it looks like a better value in price while it is going against you?
- You must be able to limit your risk exposure to your planned limit and not keep adding positions or leverage when you have reached your limit.
- What is the frequency of your trade signals?
- Are you trading enough markets or stocks to have enough diversity for ample trade opportunities and trends?
- What is the maximum drawdown you are willing to take?
- What are your targeted annual returns?
- What is the warning sign that something is wrong with your trading system?
- How many commissions will you incur monthly and annually with your system?
- Is their liquidity risk in your market?
- How much screen time do you need to execute your trades?
- How will you know that your trading methodology is not for you?

Will you take the entry?

Entry signals are useless unless you are willing or able to take them. If you are afraid, then your fear may be trying to protect you from losing money. Try trading smaller than you initially planned to see if that eases your mind. Trading is a business; you should feel serious and focused on entries but not stressed out or losing sleep. Those are warning signs that something is wrong.

If decreasing your trade size doesn't resolve your uneasiness, you may need to build more faith in your system by doing more back testing, chart studies, and coming to terms with the risks involved. Taking your buy signal requires faith in yourself and your system, and that takes patience and time. Start small and you can always increase your size as your comfort level and confidence grows.

Will you take your stop loss?
It is much easier to exit a profit taking sell signal than a stop loss sell signal. The stop loss level must be embraced when the buy signal is taken. Always consider position sizing and how much money will be lost if the stop loss is hit. Be prepared to accept that if the price can get to your stop loss level, then you are wrong.

Ego is a roadblock of stop losses. You must be able trade your plan with discipline to override your ego. Trading too large makes it difficult to take your initial stop loss because it's easier to hope that it will come back than it is to take the big loss now and accept defeat. It is easier to take a small loss than a big loss. Staying on the wrong side of a losing trade is dangerous because eventually you will be on the wrong side of a trend with a large position size, and you could lose it all.

Every profitable trader must develop the skill of accepting a loss when they have been proven wrong. Every time that you take your stop loss and your trade bounces back, you may think that you don't need stop losses and you should wait for a reversal. The reason we have stop losses is the same reason we have brakes on our cars or insurance on our homes. We may not always need them, but it is a bad idea to expose ourselves to the risk of ruin by not having that coverage the one time that we need it.

Will you position size safely and consistently?
You must consistently take your buy signals based on preplanned position sizing and not out of desperation or unfounded hope. One of the biggest pitfalls of new traders is trading too large due to overconfidence. Your position sizing must be consistent as you take your buy signals. Each position size must be inside the range of how much you are willing to risk on any one trade.

You can risk more capital on the best setups based on the risk/reward ratio and probabilities, but that may mean that you risk losing 2% of your capital when you usually risk 1%. It doesn't mean risking half or all of your capital on one big option or futures trade; that is a recipe for eventual ruin.

Can you resist adding to a losing trade?
Technical traders shouldn't have the same problems as fundamental traders. As a stock drops lower and lower, it looks like a better value for an investor, but it looks like a downtrend to a trader. All it takes are a few times when a trader finds themselves on the wrong side of a strong trend, adds to the losing trade, and finds themselves in the middle of financial and emotional ruin. A trader should trade small when losing and avoid amplifying their losses.

Will you limit your risk exposure?
Risking a 1% loss on any one trade is a great way to begin your risk management planning, but you also must consider how many trades you have at any one time, as well as their correlations to each other.
- How many entry signals can you take before you can't add any more risk?
- When should you stop taking new entry signals?
- Will you only expose your trading capital to three trades at any one time?
- Will you limit your total risk exposure to three at a time if the trades are correlated positions, like three tech stocks?
- Would you expand to five total positions if they are not closely correlated like trades in oil, gold, the U.S. Dollar, the S&P 500, and a tech stock?

You amplify your risk when you have multiple positions in the same sector or all in stocks. You can diversify your risk if you are in different markets like bonds, metals, energy, currencies, and agricultural commodities that generally don't move in the same direction at the same time. Study your markets and decide on the appropriate risk based on current correlations. Understand that correlations can change over time and during different market conditions.

How many trade signals will your system give you in your time frame?
The quantity of your trade signals will be as important as the quality of your signals. You may find a great buy signal only to discover that your signal only triggers once or twice a year. Two trades a year doesn't work for most traders. On the other side, a day trader may have too active of a signal that can cause 10 losses and 20 commissions to get in and out of trades in one day. That won't work well, either. A trader has to understand how many times a signal will trigger on average in their time frame on their watch list, and calculate the potential losses that could be caused during a losing streak while taking into account their commission costs.

If you want a 30% annual return, you may only need 60 trades a year with a 50% win rate if your winners created 2% returns, and your losers only amounted to a 1% loss on your total trading capital. Thirty wins that create a 60% return, minus thirty losing trades that create 30% in losses may be all you need. This is a basic example, but it demonstrates the big picture of trading frequency. The majority of traders have higher odds of profitability the less they trade. The more you trade, the more commission costs and bid/ask spreads you have working against you.

Do you trade enough markets for buy signal opportunities?
If you are trading trends, then you need to be trading enough markets to give yourself the potential of capturing those trends. Systematic trend following systems only work because they are trading diversified futures across all markets: metal, agricultural commodities, energy, bonds, equities, interest rates, currencies, etc. They limit their risk through diversification with small positions for each signal entry, and profit by capturing the trend in whatever market that has one.

Trend following doesn't work as well if at all when trading only one or few markets. The same thing is true for momentum stock strategies; you need a list of at least 10 to 15 stocks if you are looking to buy the ones that breakout and trend. You need to own the right one, but you have to watch enough so you don't miss that right one. For systematic trading to be successful, you need diversification of opportunities to get the buy signals you are looking for.

How much money can you handle losing?
What percentage of your trading capital are you willing to lose? If you start with $100,000 can you handle getting down to $90,000? Will you quit trading if you end up with only $80,000? It is crucial to make these decisions before you dive into real-time trading. You need to know when you should get out, and avoid your maximum loss level. Trade small enough so you never get near your breaking point. Many new traders miss this simple principle because they see the prize but not the danger. It is much easier to keep the money you have than to lose it and try to get it back. Each buy signal is an opportunity to both make money and lose money.

How much money do you intend to make trading?
Your goal for returns will correlate closely with your potential for losses. Typically, the bigger the return the greater the drawdown in capital to achieve those returns due to the increased risk. If you want to try for a 50% annual return, you will increase your potential for a 50% drawdown in that attempt. Great traders have average returns of about 20% a year with drawdowns staying under 10%.

Don't fall for promises of easy and quick millions by penny stock pushers or other trading scams, the odds are much greater that you lose all your money. Understand your goal for returns first, then work on a system that has the potential to create those returns.

How will you know something is wrong with your trading?
If you have more than 10 losses in a row early on, if your heart is pounding on entry and you stay stressed out while holding a position, or you watch every single price tick and you are not a day trader, something isn't right with your methods.

Trading isn't an extreme sport. You should be conducing business calmly; using buy signals and sell signals without drama or consternation. The best money managers and traders I know have no emotion because each trade is just one of the next 100. Celebrating a winning trade like you just won the super bowl or falling into depression over a losing trade, are warning signs that you are overly invested. Excessive losses in a row may mean that your stop losses are too tight, or you are having trouble being patient enough because it is outside your comfort zone.

How much will your buy and sell signals cost you in commissions?
An often-overlooked cost of doing business as a trader is commission costs. If you are a day trader, then you need to calculate your potential round trip commission costs for entering and exiting each trade over a day, weeks, and months. For example, if a day trader makes three trades a day, it will cost $7 on each entry then $7 on each exit. So $42 a day to execute day trades. That is $210 a week for 5-days, $840 a month for 4 weeks, and $10,920 a year. Commission costs have to be considered in the equation of being a profitable trader.

Is their liquidity risk in your market?
Before you take a buy signal on a penny stock or stock options, you must make sure the bid/ask spread is tight enough to justify the trade. Traders that buy illiquid OTC stocks, "pink sheet" stocks, or penny stocks (whatever you want to call them) can lose money instantly when getting in them if they are low volume, and you buy at the ask price and the bid is lower. Also, you can try to sell them only to find that there are no buyers. This forces you to wait and take a lower price than the bid while they try to find a buyer to purchase your penny stock.

My advice is to avoid penny stocks due to the liquidity risk. Even stock options on major stocks can have slippage on out-of-the-money options due to a lack of liquidity at that price. A $1 gap between the bid/ask spread on an option contract will cost you $100 to get in, and then $100 to get back out. The farther options go away from at-the-money strike prices, the wider the spread gets as liquidity dries up. Only trade options in the front month and close to at-the-money in major stocks to avoid the large losses in the bid/ask spread.

How much screen time do you need to execute your trades?
Your type of trade signals will dictate how much time you spend in front of the computer each day. There are many trend following systems that only require you to take your signals at the market open or at the end of the day. There are also trend following strategies with trade signals and portfolio changes that only happen at the end of the week, or even the end of the month.

Many stock investment portfolios only make moves to redistribute their portfolio allocations once a quarter. Warren Buffet may hold a stock for decades. On the other hand, a day trader may need to look at the quote screen all day waiting for his signal. Other day traders may only trade the first and last hour of the markets. Swing traders and position traders may trade once every few days or weeks. Some futures traders' trade over night as their market is open.

The important thing is to create signals that you are able to take with your current life commitments. Few people can day trade or focus closely enough on the open and close due to other commitments on their time. Find the right screen time that allows you take your singles, or use automatic buy stops and stop losses if needed.

Warning signs that something is wrong:
Big losses, ten consecutive losses, an inability to take your entries or exits, and excessive stress or emotions will tell you that something is wrong with your trading system. Revisit your position sizing, total risk exposure, time frame, stop losses, and the faith you have in yourself and your system. Usually the issues come down to trading too big and/or having to tight of a stop loss.

How will you know that your trading methodology is not for you?

To be successful over the long term, your trading has to fit your personality. Some traders love day trading and the pace of constantly monitoring quotes. Others hate day trading and it bores them or stresses them out. Some love to pick stocks and carry focused position sizes for weeks and months. To be good at trading you have to love what you do. Find a methodology you are passionate about, and one that you are willing to devote the time and energy necessary to making it a winning system.

If you need help in the areas of risk management and trader psychology, www.newtrader101.com can help.

Why you build your own signals

"Listen only to what the market is telling you now. Forget what you thought it was telling you five minutes ago. The sole objective of trading is not to prove you're right, but to hear the cash register ring." – Marty Schwartz

The purpose of creating buy and sell signals is to capture a trend's profitability inside your trading timeframe. Let's think about the creation of a trading edge and its many levels.

First, we can consider that taking trades randomly should give us a 50/50 chance of being right or wrong. If we flipped a coin before we entered a trade, half the time we should be entering in the right direction whether long or short, and price should move in our favor theoretically.

How can we improve these random odds? We can go in the direction of the trend in our time frame on the daily chart while using the weekly chart to monitor the larger trend. While the stock market has a bias to trend upwards in longer time frames, buy and hold investing is not more profitable because large profits are given back during bear markets.

Trading stocks from the long side during bull markets and removing the short side during bull markets will move the odds in your favor by better than 50%. The stock market goes up more than it goes down over long periods of time. There are more bull markets and range bound markets than downtrends, markets crashes, and bear markets. Shift to a long-only strategy during bull markets will help you develop an edge in these environments.

Contrarian traders with no valid reasons for their actions frequently miss stock market uptrends. Buy and hold investors hold their stocks during bear markets when they shouldn't and give back years of gains. Capital flows and creates trends in all markets over longer time frames, and it's much easier to go with the direction of the flow than to try to predict every turn and reversal.

The majority of profitable traders I know personally trade with a trend. The easiest way to filter a trend is using moving averages. Moving averages smooth out long-term price movement, and can show you the ascending or descending trend in your time frame. They are used in building most trading systems. Trading on the right side of the key moving averages in your time frame will give you your first edge over other traders. Your odds of being right improve to more than 50% when you systematically stay with the right moving average.

Enter with a great risk/reward ratio

Always buy with a good margin of safety. When a stock or index is in an uptrend and then pulls back to a key price support level, technical oversold level, or ascending moving average, you can enter with a stop loss that is set outside the trading range or lower than the key pullback area. The odds of your trade being a winner are greatest when the probabilities of your stop loss being hit are the lowest.

After entering in the direction of the trend, you want to be profitable before you are stopped out for a loss. Your position size has to be small enough to allow you to manage your emotions so you can stay in a trade until there is a valid reason to exit.

Your trade size has to be big enough to make a win meaningful, but small enough to not put your trading account in jeopardy. You should *never* expose yourself to the potential of large losing trades. You must be able to survive losing streaks because they will come. The simplest strategy for risk control is not to allow your losing trades to cost you more than 1% of your total trading account.

If you're trading with 10% of your total trading capital in one position, then your stop loss can be 10% below your entry for a 1% loss of total trading capital. If you're trading with 20% of your total trading capital, your stop loss should be 5% below your entry price for a 1% total trading capital loss. If you are trading with 25% of your total trading capital, your stop loss would have to be 4% below your entry price for a 1% total trading capital loss.

Part of taking an entry signal will be position sizing correctly to avoid any large losses. Not trading too big will give you an edge over traders that have to go all-in on every trade because they have small accounts. Position sizing will give you an edge over other traders and help determine your long-term success. If 1% at risk seems too small it is likely that your trading account is too small. Your trade signals will be risking a small amount trying to make a large amount.

Your stop loss is the brakes and your profit target is your destination.

Your signals will only work if you are risking a little to make a lot. If you are risking a lot to score a big win, then those risks will eventually catch up to you. Even professionals like Victor Niederhoffer, Long Term Capital Management, and Amaranth learned the lessons of the risk of ruin the hard way.

Exit when the risk is greater than the reward

The next step in our signal example is to see exactly where we would exit after our entries. Some studies by Van Tharp and Tom Basso have shown how even random entries can be profitable if the exit is managed to create big wins when the trade trends, and small losses when the trade goes in the wrong direction.

"Tom Basso designed a simple, random-entry trading system ... We determined the volatility of the market by a 10-day exponential moving average of the average true range. Our initial stop was three times that volatility reading. Once entry occurred by a coin flip, the same three-times-volatility stop was trailed from the close. However, the stop could only move in our favor. Thus, the stop moved closer whenever the markets moved in our favor or whenever volatility shrank. We also used a 1% risk model for our position-sizing system. ...

We ran it on 10 markets. And it was always, in each market, either long or short depending upon a coin flip. ... It made money 100% of the time when a simple 1% risk money management system was added. ... The system had a (trade success) reliability of 38%, which is about average for a trend-following system."

Source: Van K. Tharp, Trade Your Way to Financial Freedom

To limit randomness and create a profitable system after you enter with a trade in the direction of the trend, you will set up your sell signals to limit losses. At the same time, you should allow your winning trades to grow as big as they can before your price target is met. Trailing stops like ascending moving averages and ascending trend lines are tools to help you maximize these gains.

Reaching a price target to a descending moving average, at a round price number, or at an old price resistance is another great time to take profits off the table and look for a better risk/reward ratio for your next entry. Remember, the easiest path to profitability is to create asymmetry in your trading so you have big wins and small losses.

Another key to trading profitability will be the ability to hold a winning trade and let it go as far as possible and not exit it until there's a valid reason. Winning trades should only be exited for a reason and not an emotion. You will need the big wins to pay for all the small losses and cutting winners short will greatly hurt your profitability. Do not get out of a trade until your signal tells you to, but when it does, then get out!

How to build your own signals

"I turn bullish at the instant my buy stop is hit, and stay bullish until my sell stop is hit." – Ed Seykota

Just like builders use hammers and saws to build houses, traders use technical tools to build their own trading systems. You only need a few of these tools to begin to build your own signals, and in fact, you can have too many indicators that lead to confusion. The most important thing to keep in mind is that there is no one-size-fits-all solution. Some technical indicators work while markets are range bound and others only work during trends. Many are useless during high volatility and crashes. No indicators work in all markets or under all conditions.

Trading profitability doesn't come from a perfect indicator or a magic system, it comes from creating an edge over other traders and trading that edge to have more profits than losses over a long period of time. Your win rate will fluctuate as market conditions shift between uptrends, downtrends, range bound, and volatility.

Buy Signals

Technical indicators that can be used to build your own buy signals:
- Price
- Price versus previous day's highs and lows
- Moving averages
- MACD
- RSI
- Chart Patterns
- Trends
- Momentum
- Candlesticks
- Price gaps

Trading price action alone
Price signals can be breakouts of a price range over a set number of days, buy signals at 52-week highs, or sell short signals at 52-week lows in price. There are traders that believe price alone is the only indicator you need.

Daily price versus previous day's highs and lows

Trading today based on yesterday's low or high price range is a day trader strategy. They also may trade the intra-day range of support and resistance, buying the lows of the day or selling the high of the day short. Day traders like intra-day volatility to give them opportunity to make money intra-day on price swings and trends. Some swing traders set stops based on the high or low of the previous day's price range.

Using moving averages

Moving averages are the average of prices over a specific time frame, and they can give a trader a better overall view of a trend. They are trend following indicators and don't do well in range bound markets. Moving averages can act as entries, exits, and trailing stops. Trend following systems can be built based on moving average crossovers to create buy and sell signals. Single moving averages like the 200 and 250-day used alone in index ETFs can outperform buy and hold investing in the long term, for both higher returns and lower drawdowns in capital.

MACD as a swing trading signal

The MACD (Moving Average Convergence/Divergence) is a momentum indicator that shows the relationship between two moving averages of prices. The MACD is the difference between a 26-day and 12-day exponential moving average. A 9-day exponential moving average, called the "signal" line is plotted on top of the MACD to show buy/sell opportunities. The MACD is profitable in markets with wide swinging price ranges. It is not useful in flat or markets with very tight price ranges. I have found the MACD to be the most useful as a swing trading indicator after crossovers. The Moving Average Convergence Divergence can work to show short-term reversals inside the longer term trend for swing traders. It can be part of a filter for other signals or a signal in itself.

RSI as a profit taking strategy

Relative Strength Index (RSI) is a momentum oscillator that measures the speed and change of price movements. The RSI oscillates between 0 and 100. RSI is considered overbought when above 70 and oversold when below 30. Signals can also be generated by centerline crossovers over or under 50. Over 50 is a bullish cross and under 50 is a bearish cross. RSI can also be used to identify the general trend as greater than 50 is bullish and less than 50 is bearish. A breakout over 70 and a breakdown under 30 can also be used as a trend indicator. The Relative Strength Index can show when price has become overbought or oversold, is due for a potential reversal, or the danger of something going parabolic as it breaks out.

Chart patterns as visual trends

Chart patterns use trend lines to map out the buying and selling of market participants looking for trends and potential reversals of trends. Flags, pennants, triangles, cups and handles, are examples of connecting the lows or highs in price over a time frame to establish a trend of higher highs, lower lows, or price ranges. Chart patterns can be bullish, bearish, continuation, or reversal patterns. Chart patterns are about connecting trend lines to identify potential breakout points for an entry to capture the next trend.

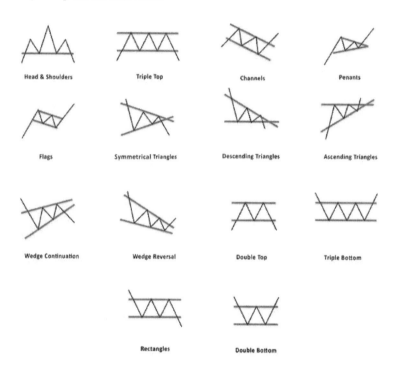

Head & Shoulders   Triple Top   Channels   Penants

Flags   Symmetrical Triangles   Descending Triangles   Ascending Triangles

Wedge Continuation   Wedge Reversal   Double Top   Triple Bottom

Rectangles   Double Bottom

Trends are your friend

Uptrends are defined as a market having higher highs and higher lows in a specific time frame.
Downtrends are defined as a market having lower highs and lower lows in a specific time frame.

Trends have to be quantified based on your trading time frame. Warren Buffet trades the longest term trend: he bets on the capitalist system always driving up the prices on the stocks of the best businesses. A day trader may only be concerned with the next hour a stock is trading. The simplest way to make money in the financial markets is to identify the trend, quantify the trend, and stay on the right side of it in your time frame. There are many ways to do this.

Momentum for fast profits
Moving fast in one direction with no sizeable pullbacks is my definition of momentum. Momentum can cut both ways leading to fast profit or fast losses. The best momentum is found at the beginning of a bull market as a stock breaks out to new all-time highs. The old all time high is likely to become the new support. The stock could go on to increase 20% in price in a month or even double that year. Momentum works at all-time highs because everyone that is holding that stock has a profit and has no pressure to sell. There is no pressure from stop losses or trailing stops, only profit taking pressure, which is usually light. Resistance levels for a stock making all-time highs tend to be whole numbers like $50 or $100 because this is where many traders set their profit targets. Momentum trading works best with new concept stocks that are innovative and have little competition.

Candlesticks are for affirmation
Candlesticks are a graphic way of depicting the opening price, closing price, and trading range on a chart that is more visual than bar charts. While they are not signals by themselves, they are great for confirmation inside the context of a chart at key levels. A bullish candle off a key support level has more meaning than a bullish candle in the middle of a strong downtrend that doesn't converge with other bullish technical indicators.

Sell Signals

When you enter a trade you will either exit with:

- A big profit
- A small profit
- Even
- A small loss
- A big loss

Technical indicators that can be used to build your own sell signals:
- Stop losses
- Price Targets
- Trailing stops
- ATR stops
- Time stops

Stop losses

The point of stop losses is to make it highly unlikely that you will have big losses. In contract markets like options, your loss is limited to your position size. In the stock market, large gaps in price at the open can bypass your stop loss and give you a bigger loss than expected. Your position size is your first line of defense against big losses, and your stop loss is the insurance policy that limits your losses as a trade goes against you.

A stop loss has to be placed outside the normal price action at a key price level that shows you are wrong, and not at the place that makes you exit out of fear. Your stop loss has to give your trade enough room and time to be right, not stopping you out before your trade is invalidated. Key places to set stop losses are a percentage below key support or resistance levels of price, moving averages, or key technical indicators like MACD crosses or moving average crossovers.

Price targets are for maximum profits on the exit

Price targets should be set at levels where your risk/reward ratio has skewed against your trade and the odds of a reversal from an extended price level is greater than the odds of it going in your favor. Price targets can be set at key round price levels at overbought/oversold oscillator levels like the 70 RSI to exit longs, the 30 RSI to exit shorts, rallies back to key price support or resistance levels, or to key moving averages.

Trailing stops allow your profits to run as far as they will go

A trailing stop is when you allow your stop loss to stay close as your trade becomes a winner. A short-term moving average is one way to do this. If your trade reverses back under the 5-day EMA or 10-day SMA you would stop out. A strong trend could use the 5-day EMA and a trade with a wider price rang could use the 10-day SMA. I like to use a close below a key moving average for my trailing stops so price confirms at the close, and I am not stopped prematurely intra-day due to noise. You should be very careful with position size based on volatility to be able to hold to the close. Another trailing stop could be a loss of the previous day's low for long positions, or the break above the previous day's high for short positions. These can be intra-day or end of day depending on your time frame.

ATR stops get you out of a trade after a few bad days
The ATR% stop method can be used for any type of trade because the width of the stop is determined by the percentage of average true range (ATR). ATR is a measure of volatility over a specified period of time. Normally a high ATR indicates a volatile market, while a low ATR indicates a less volatile market. By using a certain percentage of ATR, you ensure that your stop is dynamic and moves with market conditions. Widen your stop in more volatile times and lower it in less volatile markets to keep from being stopped out too soon and to account for noise in price movement.

- Time stops frees up your capital for better uses
- Time stops set a limit on how long you will wait for a trade to work before exiting and looking for better opportunities. It is stop loss on your opportunity cost.
- A time stop will vary greatly and may be hours for a day trader or months for a position trader.

Mechanical versus discretionary systems

In classic Star Trek, Captain Kirk believed in his ability to make the best decision in any circumstance based on his experience and cunning. Mr. Spock contrasted Kirk's style by using logic and the probabilities of success to make the best decision.

Discretionary traders are similar to Kirk. They try to get by with their experience, intuition, and wits, relying on their ability to make the right decisions in the heat of price action. Discretionary traders can have signals that are more elaborate than just price action, and can go deeper into the psychology of what other traders are thinking. A discretionary trader's methodologies may consist of *trading the trader,* anticipating the actions of shorts and longs, like professional poker players anticipate other players based on their bets.

In contrast, mechanical traders are more like Spock, only following a well researched plan for position sizing, specific entries and exits, and executing their plan based solely on market behavior and probabilities of a success outcome.

For discretionary traders a bad trade could be one where they lose money, for mechanical traders a bad trade is one where they lost discipline and failed to follow their trading plan.
Here are the differences between traders that rely on their instincts, intuition, rules, and chart reading abilities and those who are pure, mechanical, systematic traders.

Discretionary Traders trading signals are:
- Based on information flow.
- Trying to anticipate what the market will do.
- They read their own opinions and past experiences into the current market action.
- Based on what their own trading rules to govern their trading.
- Tied to their egos and the outcomes are typically tied to their emotions.
- Based on many different indicators to trade at different times. Sometimes it may be macro economic indicators, chart patterns, or even macroeconomic news.
- Generally executed on a small watch list based on their expertise of the markets they trade, or they are looking for patterns on stocks through a screening process.
- Based more on opinion, principles, and strategy than historical backtests.
- Based on creating great risk/reward ratios.
- Position sized based on the confidence they have on any one trade.

Mechanical Trader signals are based on:
- Trading price flow.
- They have no opinion about the market and are following what the market is actually doing, i.e. following the trend.
- Very strict and delineated rules to govern their entries and exits, risk management, and position size.
- Being unemotional because when they lose it is because the market was not conducive to their system, and they will win over the long-term.
- Using the exact same technical indicators for their entries and exits and they never change them. Their entries are systematic with no opinions needed, just discipline.
- Trading their technical system using price action and trends so they don't need to be an expert on the fundamentals.

While discretionary traders are busy trying to digest what fundamental news and information mean, mechanical traders are taking the signals they are getting from actual price movement in the market. Mechanical traders are not thinking and predicting what the market is going to do, they are reacting to what the majority is doing based on their predetermined system's entry signals.

For the average trader, being a 100% Mechanical System Trader usually maximizes the chance of success in the markets, especially if you are using a historically proven, profitable system. If you are removing the emotions and ego from your trading and are controlling your risk of ruin with proper trade size and stop losses, then you have a high probability of being a consistently profitable trader.

Basic signal examples

"In order of importance to me are: 1) the long-term trend, 2) the current chart pattern, and 3) picking a good spot to buy or sell." – Ed Seykota

Signals are only one third of your trading system. The other two thirds are more important; your risk management to avoid the risk of ruin for your account, and your psychology to risk your mental and emotional ruin while trading through the peaks and valleys of your equity curve.

Please trade these signals responsibly as results will vary greatly based on current market conditions.

Trend Following Signals
- Enter on a 20-day breakout in price and exit on a 10-day breakout in the opposite direction.
- Enter on a 30-day breakout in price and exit on a 15-day breakout in the opposite direction.
- Enter on a 50-day breakout in price and exit on a 25-day breakout in the opposite direction.
- Enter on a 55-day breakout in price and exit on a 20-day breakout in the opposite direction.
- Enter on a 100-day breakout in price and exit on a 50-day breakout in the opposite direction.

How do trend followers trade over many markets and consistently grow capital?
- They use proven trading systems that identify and follow trends.
- They create systems that give them entry and exit signals along with risk management parameters.
- They are not experts on the fundamentals of any market, but their systems are masters of measuring the price action in all markets.
- Their price systems work across multiple futures markets because historically, big trends happen consistently over time.
- They cut their losses short when they are incorrect but when they are right they let the winning trade run as far as possible.

- They unemotionally sell when their exit signal says the trend is coming to an end. They are content to get the meat of a trend, not buying at the low or selling at the high, but waiting for the market to tell them to get in and then when to get out.

Many traders have proven that trend following works over the long-term. The legendary Jesse Livermore and Nicolas Darvas were both trend followers who made millions by buying strong trends based on price action. Modern day professional money managers like Richard Dennis, Ed Seykota, and William O'Neal make millions trading with the trend. John W. Henry bought the Boston Red Sox with his profits from managing his trend following fund.

Trend followers don't try to predict the future; they only follow the price trend of the financial markets, and they get in or out when their system tells them to do so. They go both long and short based on their systems, with no bias to bullishness or bearishness. They may have volatility filters or a filter using a 200-day moving average for their system, but their trades are quantified rather than opinionated or predictive. While they may have steeper drawdowns in the short-term, they consistently have returns on capital in the long-term. They almost always find themselves positioned correctly on the right side of a market during fat tail events outside the normal bell curve, crashes, and panics because the market has already warned them. Most trend followers made huge returns during October of 2008 because they were already short due to the trend already in place. Trend followers made major returns in the financial panic of 2008-2009 while the majority of investors suffered heavy losses. Trend following is for long-term growth in capital by trading multiple futures markets.

Authors Micahel Covel and Andrea Clenow do a great job of documenting the long-term success of trend following funds.

Trading price ranges and buying the dip (Buy low, sell high)
- Buy a pullback to price support in your time frame sell a rally back to price resistance in your time frame.
- Buy pullbacks to the 50-day simple moving average in growth stocks in uptrends with a   price target back to the previous high price or a rally back to the 70 RSI.
- Buy pullbacks to the 200-day simple moving average with a price target back to the 50-day simple moving average.

The whole point of trading a price range is to buy when their seems to be a little fear taking price back near support, and sell a little greed as resistance is approached.

This type of trading is dependent on the specific market you are trading and it's key levels.

The following example shows how the SPY ETF stayed in a trading range for the first half of 2015. Support was revisited twice before it was lost, and resistance held twice after being established. This is a daily chart, but the principles can be applied to any time frame.

Previous support and resistance usually hold the first few tests and provide a great risk/reward ratio for selling resistance short or buying the dip back to support. The odds of having a winning trade increase if you use other filters. Selling resistance short has higher probabilities of success if combined with overbought signals like an RSI of 65-70, while buying support has higher success rates if the support aligns with a 30-35 RSI level. Once price closes above resistance or support, then the range is broken and it is considered a breakout signal. The more times support or resistance is tested, the greater the odds of it breaking.

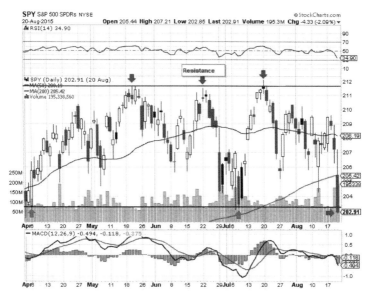

Charts courtesy of StockCharts.com.

This example shows that if you are in the right growth stock, the 50-day SMA can act as long-term support for a position trade to keep you long, your stop loss if it is lost, and a dip buying opportunity back at support. If you buy a bounce off the 50-day SMA, you can take your profits the next time it makes a new high in price or it becomes overbought.

Charts courtesy of StockCharts.com.

In range bound markets, you are looking to buy dips back to key support levels to moving averages or price levels before it breaks out to go higher or lower. Buying dips works in both range bound markets and uptrends. You are buying fear cheap and trying to sell it when some greed either takes price back to resistance or to a new high. Dip buying doesn't work in downtrends because lows tend to get lower and support levels are lost. Look for the last place that price bounced to locate your last support level. Expand your time frame to see if it has been support before. Find where the buyers were in the past to increase your odds for buying a dip.

Momentum entry signals (Buy high and sell higher)

- Buy a 52-week high in price and trail your stop with an ascending moving average (10-day EMA) or a 3 ATR. (14 day period)
- Buy a new all-time high and trail your stop with an ascending moving average (10-day EMA) or a 3 ATR. (14 day period)

Why is buying into, and holding onto all-time highs, good trading?
The more times a support or resistance level is touched by price, the stronger that level becomes. Most traders deal in range bound securities because they think they know that a stock's price is unlikely to exceed a strong resistance level. The more traders that recognize this principle, the more short sellers there are lined up to short a key resistance level like a 52-week high or an all-time high. And the more short sellers there are, the more buy stops there will be at an unlikely level, just beyond resistance by momentum traders, breakout traders, and some trend followers.
For example, if the SPY has approached the same all-time high on several occasions, profit taking has become exhausted, and investor sentiment is more positive due to central bank support of the equity markets, media induced fear has probably caused everyone that wanted to sell to already be out.

This causes:
- Demand for stocks to go up, as selling pressure dissipates and the remaining investors are just holding.
- All-time highs to be breached and, short sellers to be squeezed out as they are stopped out and forced to buy back to cover their short positions. This creates what we affectionately term a *short squeeze*. Everyone who thought they knew where the ceiling (resistance) was, no longer holds a position in that index. What once was the ceiling becomes the new floor, or support level.

Once a security breaks out above strong resistance, it takes some time to create and recognize the new ceiling. Short sellers become less likely to step in because they can no longer anticipate where the stock is likely to find resistance and reverse. The term *blue-sky breakout* is used to describe a stock that breaks above all previous resistance points. At all-time highs, there is no resistance, no stop losses being triggered, and only profit taking. There is a temporary relief of selling pressure because current holders are profitable. Price moves higher until profit targets are reached and profit taking begins again.

Trading opening price gaps up over the previous trading range
- Buy a gap up in price at the end of the day with a stop loss at the low of the gap up day.
- Use a close under the previous day's low as your trailing stop.

- Buy into a morning gap with a 1 ATR (14) as your stop loss. Take profits that day into the rally or hold it with a 2 ATR trailing stop or a close under the previous day's low.
- Generally the higher the percentage of gap above the old price, the lower the odds of a winning trade.
- Buying opening gaps in price above the previous trading range work better in bull markets and less in bear markets because stocks are under accumulation in bull markets.

When a market opens with a gap up out of a trading range it confounds many traders. They don't understand how the price can gap up to a whole new trading range, stay there all day, and even go higher through the day. If the gap is out of an oversold level, there is a high probability of trade entry as a new trading range is established with the potential of a new uptrend. If a gap up doesn't fill in the first hour and a half of trading, the odds are it will just keep going in that direction for the remainder of the day. Shorting momentum is generally a bad idea, and shorting a gap up is not a signal, it is an opinion unless the gap is into an overbought area like the 70 RSI. Gap ups tend to work better in long-term uptrends than when the market is in a downtrend.

What causes these situations? They are generally psychological and not based on fundamental valuation changes:
- Gaps in prices can be one of the strongest indicators of momentum, and while most are using gaps as an opportunity to get out of a winning trade, many times it is a great entry signal and the beginning of a strong trend in the direction of the gap.
- Gaps work best in growth stocks especially after earnings are reported when they go into an accumulation phase.
 - A gap signals momentum and that nobody was willing to make a trade in the empty gap that is created in the chart. Think about the fact that there were no bids or asks except at the opening gap price.
- Gaps can be bought at the open for a possible quick gain and good entry, but there is still a possibility that the gap could collapse violently. Better odds are to wait for the gap to hold for the first hour of trading and then make an entry. You may get a better entry on a pullback and avoid being caught if the gap fails and price collapses. I like to buy gaps at the end of the day for the highest probability that it's a gap and go, and not a gap and crap.
- Gaps in times of high volatility don't tend to hold and trend as well as a gap out of a clean price base.
- A gap off a key moving average or one that opens over a key moving average has a better chance of success than a random gap.

- A gap into all-time highs is especially powerful with all holders now profitable. The gap tends to continue with every holder letting the profits run.
- Shorts caught in gaps can add fuel to the fire of the trend as they are forced to buy to cover.
- A great place to set a stop is just under the low of the gap up day; price should not breach that level if it is going to trend. Using an end of day stop gives you better odds of not being shaken out if it just dips there temporarily.
- After the low of the day holds and a trend begins over multiple days, then the trailing stop could be moved to the 10-day EMA and then the 5-day EMA late in the trend to lock in profits, but allow the trend to continue in your favor.
- Also be aware that a momentum growth stock that gaps up don't have long-term resistance, they tend to pause and make higher highs. Overbought indicators are not helpful in analyzing momentum growth stocks under heavy accumulation by money managers.
- When caught on the wrong side of a gap, it's best to get out in the first 30 minutes. If the gap holds and makes higher highs after the first hour and thirty minutes of the trading day, it is likely to get worse as the day goes on.
Gaps have a way of leaving so many retail traders on the sidelines because they don't want to chase. Some of my biggest winners buy into gap ups with the right position sizing and let the winners run.

Moving Averages Crossover Signals
- Enter when the 5-day EMA crosses the 20-day EMA.
- Enter when the 5-day SMA crosses the 50-day SMA.
- Enter when the 10-day SMA crosses the 100-day SMA.
- Enter when the 20-day SMA crosses the 200-day SMA
- Enter when the 50-day SMA crosses the 200-day SMA.
- Exit your mutual funds and go to cash when SPY price crosses under its 200-day SMA.
- Exit your mutual funds and go to cash when SPY price crosses under its 250-day SMA.
- When trading stocks it is usually a smoother equity curve to use these crossovers systems as long-only systems.

While few systems can be built with single moving averages alone, they can be used as a tool used for filtering and trading trends in your timeframe. They work best as crossover systems where you make entry and exit decisions when a shorter term moving average crosses over a longer term one, or you use the 200-day SMA as a filter and take long signals above that line or short signals below it. Using a loss of the SPY 200-day SMA to exit your stock mutual funds in your retirement account can dramatically reduce your drawdowns during bear markets.

5-day EMA: Measures the short-term time frame. This is support in the strongest uptrends. This line can only be used successfully in low volatility trends.

10-day EMA: "The 10-day exponential moving average (EMA) is my favorite indicator to determine the major trend. I call this 'red light, green light' because it is imperative in trading to remain on the correct side of a moving average to give you the best probability of success. When you are trading above the 10-day, you have the green light, and you should be thinking buy. Conversely, trading below the average is a red light. The market is in a negative mode, and you should be thinking sell." – Marty Schwartz

21 day EMA: This is the intermediate term moving average. It is generally the first line of support in a volatile uptrend.

50-day SMA: This is the line that strong leading stocks typically pullback to. This is usually the support level for stocks in strong uptrends.

100-day SMA: This is the line that provides the support between the 50-day and the 200-day. If it doesn't hold as support, the 200-day generally is the next stop.

200-day SMA: Bulls like to buy dips above the 200-day moving average, while bears sell rallies short below it. Bears usually win and sell into rallies below this line as the 200-day becomes resistance, and bulls buy into deep pullbacks to the 200-day when the price is above it. This line is one of the biggest signals in the market telling you which side to be on. Bull above, Bear below. Bad things happen to stocks and markets when this line is lost.

Staying on the right side of the key moving average in your time frame will give you an edge over randomness because you will be going in the direction of the price trend. Mechanical crossover systems can be created for entry and exit signals both long and short.

RSI Signals
During uptrends, the 30-35 RSI range on the daily chart presents good risk/reward opportunities for buying the dip. The stop loss is a close under the 30 RSI. Profit target is the 50 RSI.
When the RSI is in the 65-70 range, it is considered overbought and can provide good risk/reward opportunities for selling short. Buy to cover with a close over the 70 RSI. Profit target is the 50 RSI

- A break over the 50 RSI is bullish.
- A break under the 50 RSI is bearish.
- Downtrends tend to trade under the 50 RSI while uptrends tend to trade over the 50 RSI.
- A close under the 30 RSI opens the possibility of a parabolic downtrend.
- A close over the 70 RSI opens the possibility of a parabolic uptrend.

The RSI is a technical momentum oscillator that compares the amount of recent gains to recent losses to try to read the overbought and oversold levels of a market's price action. The RSI has a range of 0 to 100. A market is supposed to be overbought with a reading of 70. For traders, this is an indication that it may be time to sell their long positions at this level. The RSI at 30 is supposed to signal that an asset is starting to be oversold, and may present a good risk/reward ratio to go long at that level.

Centerline crosses at the 50 can be used as the beginning of a trend in the direction of the break (+50 bullish / -50 bearish). The traditional use of the RSI for swing trading is best used in stock indexes. The 65-70 range indicates overbought and time to exit longs. The 30-35 range indicates oversold and a potential buy signal. The RSI oscillator works best for swing trading in range bound markets. It doesn't work well for indicating extremes in trending markets, as higher highs or lower lows continue for extended periods.

The RSI is best used in combination with other indicators. A confirmation of a 30 RSI near a key support level like the 200-day SMA increases the odds of the signal working.

MACD Signals
- When the MACD line crosses over the signal line it is buy signal.
- When the MACD line crosses below its signal line it is sell signal.

The MACD is a technical indicator that attempts to measure momentum of a market's price action. It converts two moving averages into two lines on a chart by subtracting the longer term moving average from the shorter term moving average. The MACD shows the relationship between two moving averages.

The formula the MACD uses to calculate its lines comes from the 26-day exponential moving average, and the 12-day exponential moving average of a market. The 26-day EMA is subtracted from the 12-day EMA to create a line. Then the 9-day EMA of the MACD is placed with the sum of the first lines to create signals for entries and exits based on crossovers. The second line is used as a signal line as it crosses over the first.

MACD is about the relationship between two intermediate term moving averages. Its signals are based off of convergences and divergences of these moving averages. The convergence of its lines indicates the likelihood that a market is in a trading range. A divergence of the two lines as they move away from each other occurs during trends in that market.

The MACD is primarily used for swing trading signals on crossovers of the MACD line over the signal line. The MACD is not useful for identifying overbought and oversold markets as it is a measurement of convergence and divergence of two moving averages around a '0' line.

MACD can work as a standalone indicator in markets with wide price swings, but the probability of success increases when it is used with other technical indicators for confirmation.

The MACD also has a histogram in the indicator box along with the two lines. The histogram is calculated by subtracting the 9-day EMA line from the MACD-line. The slope of the histogram above or below the '0' line is a sign of the trend of the market. The histogram above zero shows upwards momentum and below '0' shows downtrend potential.

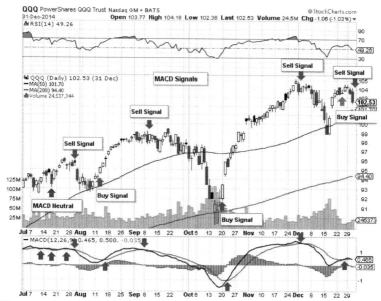

Charts courtesy of StockCharts.com.

Basic system examples

"The "easier money" in this difficult business of professional speculation is following the path of least resistance until that path has changed." – Richard Weissman

Simple signals for beating buy and hold investing:

The most popular and most promoted system for stock market participation is buy and hold investing. Investors buy mutual funds by dollar cost averaging in to them and holding them for decades. Their only sell signals are to rebalance their portfolio either quarterly or annually, and to slowly move into bonds as their retirement approaches. Meanwhile, the investors are taking on all the risk while the mutual fund managers and mutual fund companies are getting paid to underperform their benchmark indexes.

The problem with buy and hold is the huge drawdowns during bear markets and financial crises that can stay underwater for decades. While buy and hold is great in theory, most investors can't hold through big drops in their portfolio value and may end up having to sell at the wrong time. They don't know when to get back in and eventually get trapped on the sidelines.

Here are four very simple trading strategies with buy and sell signals that can replace buy and hold investing:

From January 3, 2000 to October 20, 2015 $SPY buy and hold returned 98.9% with a 55.2% drawdown. These are long only systems for beating buy and hold investing using the SPY ETF (S&P 500 index tracker) as our stock market proxy and simple moving averages as signals.

- If we traded SPY using the 200-day SMA as an end of day buy/sell indicator from January 3, 2000 to October 20, 2015, the 200-day SMA returns were 96.1% with a 27.3% drawdown. We cut the drawdown in half from the buy and hold system. This reduces the pain of drawdown dramatically by simply having a stop loss sell signal for our equity positions.

- If we traded SPY using the 250-day SMA as an end of day buy/sell indicator from January 3, 2000 to October 20, 2015, the 250-day SMA returns were 120.5% with a

23.1% drawdown. We cut the drawdown in half and actually increased the return versus a buy and hold system that used SPY. We moved or stop loss further out so we were not stopped out prematurely on noise around the 200-day, and picked up more on the bounce back over the 200-day. We stayed out of the worst bear markets and were quick to get back into rallies early when price broke back over the 250-day.

- If we traded SPY using the 20/200-day crossover as an end of day buy/sell indicator from January 3, 2000 to October 20, 2015, the 20-day/ 200-day SMA crossover returns were 173.6% with a 17.3% drawdown. We cut the drawdown in half and almost doubled the return of buy and hold investing in SPY. This system gives us a buy signal when the 20-day crosses over the 200-day and a sell signal when the 20-day crosses back under the 200-day. The 20-day acts as a filter on the 200-day, keeping us in our positions longer before exiting and waiting for more confirmation with the 20-day before we get back in. It dramatically reduces the trading activity we would experience with the 200-day alone by filtering out much of the noise.

- If we traded SPY using the 50/200-day crossover as an end of day buy/sell indicator from January 3, 2000 to October 20, 2015, the 50-day/ 200-day SMA crossover returns were 204.2% with a 17.3% drawdown. We cut the drawdown by over one third and more than doubled our returns versus just buying and holding SPY. This system gives us a buy signal when the 50-day crosses over the 200-day, and a sell signal when the 50-day crosses back under the 200-day. The 50-day acts as a filter on the 200-day keeping us in our positions longer before exiting and waiting for more confirmation with the 50-day before we get back in after being stopped out. It reduces trade signals even more than the trading activity we would experience with the 20/200-day cross, by filtering out most of the noise in the past 15 years and catching almost all significant moves up in price. Trading the 50-day crossing over the 200-day is called the golden cross and is very bullish, while the 50-day crossing under the 200-day is said to be bearish. This backtest shows this to be true in the SPY.

These back tests were done at www.ETFreplay.com.

The Legendary Turtle Traders System

Have you ever heard of the legendary Turtle traders? Millionaire trader Richard Dennis set out to find out if traders were just born to trade, or if they could be trained to be successful in the markets.
The answer? If they could follow rules they could be successful.

"I always say that you could publish my trading rules in the newspaper and no one would follow them. The key is consistency and discipline. Almost anybody can make up a list of rules that are 80% as good as what we taught our people. What they couldn't do is give them the confidence to stick to those rules even when things are going bad." –Richard Dennis: Founder of the 'Turtle Traders'.

The Turtle system proved that traders could be trained. The traders that followed the rules went on to be millionaires and to manage money professionally. Their rules were made public many years ago, and here is a brief explanation of their buy signals and sell signals:

Markets – What to buy or sell
- The Turtles traded all major futures contracts, metals, currencies, and commodities.
- The turtles traded multiple markets to diversify risk.

Position Sizing – How much to buy or sell
- Turtle position sizing was based on a market's volatility using the 20-day exponential moving average of the true range.
- The Turtles were taught to trade in increments of 1% of total account equity.

Entries – Buy signals and sell signals
- The Turtles traded a Donchian breakout system, System 1 entered a 20-day breakout and System 2 entered a 55-day breakout.
- Positions were added to in a winning trend. (Pyramiding)

Stops – When to get out of a losing position
- System 1 exited at a 10-day breakout in the opposite direction of the entry and System 2 exited at a 20-day breakout in the opposite direction of the entry.
- No trade could incur more than a 2% equity risk, stop losses and position sizing were planned accordingly

Tactics – How to buy or sell

- The most important aspects of successful trading are confidence, consistency, and discipline.
- The Turtles believed that successful traders used mechanical trading systems.
- They traded liquid markets only.

Simple trend following systems

Here are three basic trend following strategies for trading a diversified futures portfolio.

Entries and Exits:

- Enter on 30-day breakout/ Exit on a 15-day breakout in opposite direction
- Enter on 50-day breakout/ Exit on a 25-day breakout in opposite direction
- Enter on 100-day breakout/ Exit on a 50-day breakout in opposite direction

Stop loss: A filter to reduce drawdowns: 3 ATR stop based on the past 100-days.

30/15-day breakout

This type of system is based on the concept of trading a large diversified futures portfolio across all different categories; metals, energy, rates, equities, agricultural commodities, and currencies. The position sizing for this strategy should be small enough to limit risk to no more than 1% of total trading capital on any one losing trade. Profitability is based on the probability that one market will break and trend strongly to offset losses.

This is a trend following breakout system where your buy signal is a new 30-day breakout high price, and your sell short signal is a new 30-day breakdown to a low in price. This means you are buying a new 30-day high in price or selling short a new 30-day low in price. There are two potential sell signals for this strategy. The traditional strategy is to maximize the ability to capture the trend by selling your long positions with any new 15-day low in price. This acts as your stop loss if it fails to trend, or a trailing stop if it continues to trend after your entry and you were in a profitable trade. The second potential exit strategy is to set your stop loss from your entry signal at three ATRs over a 100-day period. The ATR is a trailing stop, so as volatility contracts or expands, your stops gets wider or tighter each day.
The ATR acts as a tighter stop loss on your entry, because it will take you out in a matter of a few days if the trend reverses, and lock in more profits late in a trend by taking you out much faster. The downsides to the ATR stop is that you can be stopped out of a trend faster and miss some larger trends by being shaken out prematurely on pullbacks. You have to choose whether to risk more and attempt to maximize gains, or be willing to give up some returns to reduce your drawdown.

The other two trend following systems work the same as the original example just on different timeframes.

50/25-day breakout
The buy signal is a new 50-day high in price while the sell signal is a new 25-day low in price. The sell short signal is a new 50-day low in price and the buy to cover signal is a new 25-day high in price.

100/50-day breakout
The buy signal is a new 100-day high in price while the sell signal is a new 50-day low in price. The sell short signal is a new 100-day low in price and the buy to cover signal is a new 50-day high in price.
Once again I would like to reiterate that this system requires very small position sizes to limit the potential for losses if the trend reverses soon after entry. Any one-position size is dependent on the volatility of the market you are trading, but a maximum position size would be between 0.2% of trading capital to 2% in most circumstances using this system. This is not a trade big to get rich system, it's profitability is based on diversification across multiple markets and uncorrelated positions with long-term capital growth by being exposed to the right trends.

These trading systems were fully back tested and examined in Andreas Clenow's book "Following the Trend" Check out his book for a step-by-step guide.

Be a better trader

In the New Trader 101 e-course, you'll get:

-13 high quality videos covering how and why to trade
-Real trade examples with detailed charts
-An active member forum with hundreds of ongoing conversations
Visit www.newtrader101.com and join other traders just like you!

Did you enjoy this Book?
Please consider writing a review.

Read more of our bestselling titles:

New Trader 101
Moving Averages 101
Trading Habits
Calm Trader

Printed in Great Britain
by Amazon